LIVING BEYOND OUR MEANS

The Extravagance of Biblical Stewardship

Introduction
by Carol Duerksen

A number of years ago, our church denomination was having a fund-raising campaign titled "A Call to Kingdom Commitments." At the time, I owned a time share in Bella Vista, Arkansas, and was having second thoughts about the amount of money I was paying for that in relation to our use of it. I realized I'd rather be giving the $100 a month to the stewardship campaign. But time shares are difficult—some would say almost impossible—to sell.

I remember the exact place on the country road where I was jogging when I made a deal with God: "You help me sell the time share, and you get the money."

I contacted a friend who already owned a time share at Bella Vista, hoping she might know of someone else who would be interested in ours. When she found out which week I owned, she simply said, "I think we'd be interested in that."

Within weeks the deal was closed. Suddenly I had an "extra" $100 a month. The thought crossed my mind to "forget" about the deal with God—I could find other places for the money. But I was so amazed at what had happened, I was thrilled to commit that money to the fund-raising campaign.

Some time later, my husband and I had the opportunity to buy a farm of our own. It meant increased monthly payments. Surely God would understand if I needed that $100 a month. How was I supposed to keep that up *and* help buy a farm? My excuses were pretty good, I figured.

But I couldn't forget God's faithfulness, and my promise. We bought the farm, I kept giving the $100 to God's kingdom, and there was enough money to go around.

At some point, I incorporated the $100 into a giving plan of a certain percentage each year. There were challenges along the way. As a freelance writer, I can get a call at any time from a client saying, "We don't want to do our newsletter anymore." And with that call goes income I'd been counting on.

But at least once, a "thank you so much, good-bye" call came in the morning, and in the afternoon the phone rang "out of the blue" with someone inquiring about me doing their newsletter.

"Out of the blue"? I don't think so.

I believe that when we accept God's invitation to take on stewardship as a lifestyle, God takes the trip with us. It's a trip beset by the joyful extravagance of "living beyond our means," living beyond our material possessions, *toward God*, toward a goal that doesn't end in material *stuff*.

I share this story because someone else shared his stewardship story with me. More than any Scripture passage or sermon, his story of taking risks, and God's faithfulness, is what motivated me to give it a try. Sometimes you have to hear from someone who's "been to the banquet" (see session 5) before you'll be intrigued with going yourself.

My hope for the youth who go through these sessions is that they will want to go to the banquet. I hope they will understand that stewardship involves spending our lives to "further the kingdom of God." Stewardship is an attitude. It means living as if we know we have received a great gift from God, and are eager to share it with others because there's so much. I hope they will learn that we are caretakers, not owners, of those gifts. If they'll give stewardship a try, individually or as a group, perhaps they'll begin to catch on to the fun it can be. Role models will help. If you as the leader tell your stories of taking risks as a steward, and/or explore new ways of making stewardship a lifestyle, it'll make a big difference in your youth.

Speaking from personal experience, it may even make a difference in you.

> **EXTENDER SESSION**
>
> Extender sessions suggest special activities related to the issue of the unit. They help accommodate the diversity of congregational schedules. Since each unit is undated, youth may study units in their entirety and still participate in special events of the congregation that get scheduled simultaneously with Bible study time. Extender sessions can be used anytime, but the one for this unit best follows **session 1** (if you use *Option A*) or **session 4** (if you use *Option B*). Calculate now whether or not you will be using the extender session.

ABOUT THE UNIT WRITER

Carol Duerksen is a full-time freelance writer and lives on a farm near Goessel, Kansas. She co-edits *With Magazine*, writes curriculum and newsletters, and is co-authoring a series of Amish novels with her husband Maynard Knepp. Carol and Maynard are youth leaders and teachers at Tabor Mennonite Church.

THE TEACHING PLAN
The parts of the session guide

Faith story. The session is rooted in this Bible passage.

Faith focus. The story of the passage in a nutshell.

Generation Y sidebar. Who are youth today? What do they need? What are they saying? What issues affect their lives? How do they react under certain circumstances?

Session goal. The entire session is built around this goal. What changes—in knowledge, attitude, and/or action—do you desire in your group?

Materials needed and advance preparation. This is what you will need if the session is to go smoothly. You'll feel more at ease if you've taken care of these details before you meet your group.

From life to Bible to life

The teaching plan is called *life-centered*. However, when we write each session, we always begin with Scripture. We ask, what does this particular passage say, especially to youth? Each session moves from life to Bible to life. So the Bible is really at the center of this way of teaching.

In every session we try to hit upon a tough question that youth might ask. Find out what questions on this issue are important for your group. Feel free to bring your own input and invite your group members to add their own experiences.

TEACHING THE SESSION

The five step-by-step movements will carry you from *life to the Bible and back to life*. Each session takes about 45 to 50 minutes. If there is a reproducible sheet for the session, take note of any complementary activities and stories.

1. **Focus.** Intended to create a friendly climate within the group and to *draw attention* to the issue.

2. **Connect.** Invites youth to *express* their own life experience about the issue, through talking, drawing, role playing, and other activities. Also uses memory, reason, or imagination to get the group thinking about *why* they view the issue the way they do.

3. **Explore the Bible.** What does the Bible *say* about the issue? With a minimum of lecturing, dig into the faith story and search for answers to questions raised in the first activities. The Insights from Scripture section will help clarify the faith story. Help youth discover how the faith community understands the Bible passage.

4. **Apply** the faith story. What does the Bible passage *mean* for contemporary life? This is the "aha!" moment when youth realize the faith story has wisdom for *their* lives.

5. **Respond.** Why does the Bible passage *matter*? What will the group do about the issue in light of what they have learned from their own experiences set alongside the faith story? How can we *live* the faith story rather than pass it off as a mere intellectual exercise?

LOOK AHEAD
Here are reminders for what you need to do for the next session or two.

INSIGHTS FROM SCRIPTURE
Here is a resource for Explore the Bible. Don't try to use all the material given. Take what you need to lead the session and answer questions your group may have. Let the Insights section inspire you to think and study more about the passage for the session.

REPRODUCIBLE SHEETS
Occasionally, the writer will provide a reproducible sheet to complement your session. If you choose to use this, make enough copies for the group in advance of the session. These sheets may include questions, stories, agree/disagree exercises, charts, pictures, and other materials to stimulate thinking and discussion.

Generally, no youth preparation is required unless the session plan calls for you to contact selected group members for specific tasks.

Session 1

HOW TO TREAT A LOANER

Materials needed and advance preparation
1. Contact youth in advance and tell them to bring a wrapped present for themselves to the session (details in *Option A* in Apply).
2. Pencils/pens and writing paper
3. Bibles
4. Reproducible sheets for session 1
5. Thank-you notes (*Option A* in Respond)

KEY VERSES
God blessed them, and God said to them, "Be fruitful and multiply, and fill the earth and subdue it; and have dominion over the fish of the sea and over the birds of the air and over every living thing that moves upon the earth." God said, "See, I have given you every plant yielding seed that is upon the face of all the earth, and every tree with seed in its fruit; you shall have them for food." (Genesis 1:28-29)

FAITH STORY
Genesis 1, Genesis 2:8-9, 15-24

FAITH FOCUS
Both biblical accounts of the creation of the earth emphasize that God created everything, then "loaned" it to human beings to use and enjoy. As the maker of earth and life, God "owns" the world. Though God gave this gift to humans, true ownership of the earth does not lie in who possesses it.

SESSION GOAL
In an era when ownership of things is of prime importance, instill in youth the idea that all they have is a "loaner" from God, and encourage them to live with this attitude.

TEACHING PLAN

1. FOCUS
5-7 minutes
"Let Me Tell You About My…"
Ask youth to "take inventory" of themselves, what they're wearing and have with them right now. Have them choose *one* aspect or thing they consider valuable, and tell the group about it. For example: "Let me tell you about this shirt. I love this shirt. It cost a lot, but my mom knew I wanted it so she got it for me." Or, "Let me tell you about this picture in my wallet. Well, you can probably guess why I have a picture of her in my wallet—no, she's not my sister!" (You get the picture?)

Note: If your group is large, break into groups of five, so everyone has a chance to share.

2. CONNECT
7-10 minutes
Top Ten List of MVS
Ask each youth to make a Top Ten List of the <u>M</u>ost <u>V</u>aluable <u>S</u>tuff in their life. The list can include things, people, hobbies—anything they consider important to them.

Then ask them to make a Top Ten List of *God's* <u>M</u>ost <u>V</u>aluable <u>S</u>tuff. No cop-outs here!

4

They must come up with ten things that they think God owns and would consider valuable.

Discuss their lists. Was it hard to come up with things that belong to God? If so, why? If they stated that God owns everything, ask them if they really believe that. (Save the lists for use later in the session.)

3. EXPLORE THE BIBLE
10-15 minutes

Shift to this activity by saying: *We've identified some things that we say belong to us and are valuable to us. We've named what we think belongs to God. But can we truly separate what's really ours and what's really God's?*

If you can, do either of these activities outdoors! Enjoy the natural setting as you ask for volunteers or assign parts on the reproducible sheet or in the Bible.

Option A: Hand out the skit on the reproducible sheet, call for volunteers or assign parts, and draw attention to the places in the skit where the whole group participates.

Depending on your group and time, either divide into small groups to discuss the questions and report back, or discuss them as an entire group. In question 2, the one-shoe-off option is only for those who can explain why. Don't let them cop out with "I don't know." Make them think about it and take a stand.

Option B: Assign youth to read the creation story, dividing it into the following segments: Gen. 1:1-5, 6-8, 9-13, 14-19, 20-23, 24-25, 26-31; Gen. 2:8-9 and 15-24. Pause after each segment, and ask the group to summarize what happened in that passage. Then ask:

1. *What did Adam and Eve own?*
2. *Where did they get the things they needed for life?*
3. *Do you believe that everything you have is a gift from God? If you believe that statement, take your shoes off.*
   *If you **don't** really buy that idea, keep your shoes on.*
   *If you are somewhere in the middle, **and can explain why**, take **one** shoe off.*

4. APPLY
10-15 minutes

Option A: Tell youth to pull out the presents they brought for themselves. The gift can be something they've been wanting—a special CD, item of clothing—that they go ahead and buy, OR it can be symbolic of something or someone that they consider a gift in their lives—a special pet, car, sheet music to symbolize their involvement in music, sports item, etc.

Have each person write *on their own presents* "To: (their name) From: God." Then take turns going around the group and opening the gifts. Have youth explain how it feels to think that this gift is from God. *Do you feel good or uncomfortable about what you "gave your-*

GENERATION Y
expects...
- to earn more money than their parents (87%)
- to have a better standard of living than their parents (87%)
- to have more leisure time than their parents (82%)
- to spend more time helping others (85%)

excerpted from *Youthviews*, March 1996

self"? Do you know deep down that it really belongs to God? If so, is it possible that God might have wanted it to go to someone else who needs it more than you do?

> We have a
>   beautiful mother
> Her green lap
>   immense
> Her brown
>   embrace eternal
> Her blue body
>   everything
>   we know.
>
> — Alice Walker

Option B: Ask youth to pick one thing from their Top Ten List (from Connect) and circle it. Then take turns going around the group, with each person sharing which item they chose and answering the same questions as listed in *Option A* above.

5. RESPOND
5-7 minutes

Option A: Hand out thank-you cards to each person. Have them write a note to God, listing the gifts they want to thank God for. Close with prayer (see end of *Option C*).

Option B: Challenge youth to "thank without ceasing" for the next 24 hours. This means to offer a quick prayer of thanksgiving to God for everything they think of, see, or do during that time frame. Make note of the youth who are willing to commit to activity, and check in with them later to see how it went. Close with prayer (see end of *Option C*).

Option C: Ask youth to pick a different item from their Top Ten List (other than the one they used in Apply *Option B* above) and answer the question: *If this really comes from God, how does it affect what you'll do with it?*

Close with this short prayer, or one of your own:

All good gifts around us are sent from heaven above.
God, help us to live according to this truth.
AMEN.

INSIGHTS FROM SCRIPTURE

We sing songs that say "All good gifts around us are sent from heaven above," or "Praise God from whom all blessings flow."

But do we really mean it? Do we really believe that all we have is a gift from God? Where does the Bible say so?

The Beginning is a good beginning. In the Genesis 1 and 2 passages, we see that God created everything. Then, having put it all together, including human beings, God said to those two people: "Here. The world is yours to use and enjoy, but be sure to take care of it."

Not only was humanity given the responsibility of taking care of their natural environment, but they were given each other to love and care for as well. What greater gift could a person receive?! The joy of having family and friends to love and receive love from is invaluable.

Yet too often we take them for granted. We look instead to material possessions and power to make us happy, or to make life meaningful. Youth see adults striving for wealth and success, often at the expense of time for family and personal growth. They follow the pattern we as adults model.

In the "Party in a Park" skit on the reproducible sheet, God discusses birthday gifts with Adam and Eve. Like teenagers of today, they're hoping for a car, nice clothes, money. And as you might expect from the God of eternity, God's trying to communicate that gifts such as the environment and people are so much more valuable. God's closing statement, "Or maybe you were expecting too little?" sums it up.

Revisit the idea of ownership

The other concept to work into this session is that after God has given us the gifts, they are not ours to do with as we please. We are caretakers—of the environment, of the creatures, of each other. We have been entrusted with them; in a sense they are "on loan from God." Just because we have them doesn't mean we own them. Conversely, ownership does not always lie in possession. For youth living under the pressure of a consumer society, stewardship asks them not only to take care of what they have, but to reconsider their attitude about what ownership means.

Not everyone has been given the same amount of things to care for. Where we were born—what part of the world, which community, in what family setting—all determines what we receive and what we are responsible for. Those who have been given much will be expected to be good stewards of much as well.

One option in the extender session in this unit is on the environment. If you plan to use it, do it in conjunction with or following this session. God gave us quite a park to live, work and play in, but it carries with it some major upkeep responsibilities. We can't just run around and trash the place. The stories of the goodness of creation remind us that in this world we truly are "living beyond our means" in that God has given us something we could not otherwise have created for ourselves.

> **LOOK AHEAD**
> One option in the Respond section for next session calls for a large piece of bright poster paper.

> People who seek simplicity and peace learn to choose between what is urgent and what can wait; between what is of great value and what is of little consequence.
>
> They learn the art of selective procrastination—putting off indefinitely what they never really needed to do at all.
>
> adapted from Dr. Dale E. Turner's *The Joys of Simplicity*

party in a park

GOD: Hey you two! Whatcha doing?
ADAM: Uh, not much. Just walking around, checking out this big park!
GOD: You like it?
EVE: Yeah, it's pretty cool.
GOD: Good. Very good. (*God looks at rest of the group and signals them to surprise Adam and Eve.*)
GROUP: Surprise! Surprise! Happy Birthday!
ADAM: (*looking around*) Hey, what's going on?
GOD: Don't you know? It's your birthday! Eve's too! We're having a surprise birthday party!
EVE: It is? We are? (*pauses, then asks*) How old am I?
GOD: Well, what's a good age? How about 16?
EVE: Okay. How about him? (*looks over at Adam*)
ADAM: I want to be older. I'll take 17.
GOD: Fine with me. Emotionally, that puts you at about the same age anyway. (*looks at Adam*) Sorry, guy, but that's just the way it is.
ADAM: Thanks a lot.
GOD: Anyway, let's get on to the fun stuff. Presents. But before that, shouldn't we sing? (*motions to group*)
GROUP: Sing the traditional Happy Birthday song. Or change it to something more fun, like:
Happy birthday to you, dude.
You live in zoo.
Your neighbors are monkeys,
Don't you act like one too.
EVE: Okay, now we've had the song. What's this about presents?
GOD: You know, gifts. Things I give you that you can use and enjoy.
ADAM: Let's do it.
GOD: Well, actually, I already have.
EVE: Huh?
GOD: I've given you the presents already. You're in one of them.
ADAM: We are? (*looks around*) What are we in? Just this big beautiful park!
GOD: You got it.
ADAM: This park? Mine? Um, if you don't mind me asking, but what *for*?
GOD: For everything you need. Food, water, a place to live, sunshine—what more could you want?
ADAM: A Camaro?
GOD: You in a hurry to get someplace? What's wrong with your feet?
EVE: Well, for one thing, we're barefoot.
GOD: I know. You each want a pair of new Nikes.
EVE: That'd be great. And about eating the food in this park....
GOD: Yes?
EVE: Well, from what I've seen, it's a bit heavy on the fruits and vegetables.
GOD: They're good for you.
EVE: No pizza?
GOD: I suppose if you wait long enough, there'll be a Pizza Hut here. They're popping up everywhere.
ADAM: So, let me get this right. Our birthday present is this park, a pair of Nikes, and the promise of a future Pizza Hut.
GOD: Well, a couple more things.
ADAM: (*whispers to Eve*): I was hoping so!
GOD: I gave you life, and I gave you each other.
ADAM: Well, that's kinda taken for granted....
GOD: Less than a day old, and you're already taking your life for granted? Think about the options. What if you didn't have life?
ADAM: Guess I'd be dead. A bunch of dirt.
GOD: Or what if you were all alone? What if I hadn't made this fine young woman for you? Believe me, the more time you spend with her and the more you get to know her, the more you'll be thanking me!
EVE: Yeah, Adam! Get a life!
ADAM: Okay, okay. I guess I was expecting too much when I thought you were giving us some nice presents. Cash. A hot car. Clothes. That kind of thing.
GOD: Or maybe you were expecting too little?

QUESTIONS

1. What do you suppose God meant by "Maybe you were expecting too little"?
2. Do you really believe that everything you have is a gift from God?
If you believe that statement, take your shoes off.
If you don't really buy that idea, keep your shoes on.
If you are somewhere in the middle, *and you can explain why*, take one shoe off.

Copyright © 1996 by Faith & Life Press and Brethren Press. Permission is granted to photocopy this handout for use with session 1.

Session 2

USE IT OR LOSE IT

KEY VERSE

His master said to him, "Well done, good and trustworthy slave; you have been trustworthy in a few things, I will put you in charge of many things; enter into the joy of your master." (Matthew 25:23)

FAITH STORY

Matthew 25:14-29

FAITH FOCUS

The parable of the talents highlights the responses of three slaves who were entrusted with varying amounts of money in the absence of their master. To the master's delight, two of the slaves invested the money and doubled the return, but the third, who was afraid to risk the money, was stripped of his responsibility. God requires that we develop, use, and share our abilities and financial resources, not hide them in the ground.

SESSION GOAL

As youth are choosing where to apply themselves, encourage them to develop, use and share the gifts they've received from God with the church family.

TEACHING PLAN

1. FOCUS
5-10 minutes

Option A: Ask youth to think of one thing they do well, and of an animal that symbolizes that particular skill or ability. Pass out paper and pencils, and have each person choose whether to act out or draw their animal and see if the rest of the group can guess the animal and the special ability.

Alternative: If you think your youth may have difficulty identifying their own skills, and if the group members know each other, ask them to do this activity for each other. For example, Bob would decide what to affirm in Sue, and draw or act out an animal symbolizing her talent. Have the group guess what it is.

2. CONNECT
5-7 minutes

Ask each person to complete the following: *If I could have any thing or any skill at all, I would like_____.* (Note: they can't name money itself.) Allow a few moments for thinking, then share answers.

Then go around the group one more time, this

Materials needed and advance preparation
1. Writing paper and pens/pencils
2. Bibles (at least four)
3. Copies of reproducible sheet for session 2
4. Chalkboard/chalk or newsprint/markers
5. Bright-colored poster paper cut into puzzle shapes (*option* in Respond)

time asking: *If your rich grandma died and left you $10,000, what would you do with it?*

3. EXPLORE THE BIBLE
10-15 minutes

Shift to this activity by saying: *We know that we each have things we can do well. There are also some things we wouldn't mind adding to our resume of abilities, and some items we'd like to own if we could. Jesus told a story about this.*

Pass out Bibles, and ask people to read the parts of the narrator, the master, and the three servants in Matthew 25:14-29.

Then pass out the reproducible sheets, and ask four people to read the scenarios. Discuss what happened in each story. How does your group feel about the actions of Carlos, Mandy, Damien, and Allison? What do all four have in common? What did they miss out on? What do they have in common with the third steward in the Bible story? Can your youth see themselves acting like any of these people in any way?

Refer to the discussion you had about Grandma's $10,000. Did any of them say they'd put it in savings and *never* take it out? Probably not.

4. APPLY
10-15 minutes

Refer the group to the first question you asked in the Connect section, where they named "If I could have anything at all...." Say: *Imagine you got what you wished for, but were then told you couldn't use it. What would you think about that?* The youth will probably say that would be stupid, or what's the point of having something if you can't use it. When they come up with those answers, tell them they have picked up the point precisely.

Hand out writing paper and a pencil to each person, and ask them to write their name at the top along with the skill or ability they named earlier in the session. Then pass the papers to the left, and have everyone add a skill or ability they see in that person. Continue until everyone has added something to the others' lists. At the end everyone should have their own list. (Note: Break into groups of four if you have a large group. If you have just one or two people, pass the papers around at least twice.)

Discuss: *What reasons do we come up with for not sharing our abilities with others? With our church family? Are we scared? Afraid of criticism? Think we're not good enough? Say we don't have time? There's no place to use that talent?*

5. RESPOND
5-7 minutes

Cut your bright-colored poster paper into a puzzle, making as many pieces as there are youth in the session. Give each person a piece, and ask them to write down one of the talents from their list that they are willing to

---

GENERATION Y
gets parabled...

A new program inspired by the parable of the talents has been implemented by On Earth Peace Assembly. Thirty-five young adults who have attended Peace Academies or have been members of Youth Peace Travel teams or Journey of Young Adults teams were sent $10 or $20 bills that were donated by OEPA board members. The recipients are charged with the goal of increasing the funds at least ten-fold, and returning the raised money to OEPA by a certain time. OEPA suggested holding car washes, bake sales, peace-a-thons, work projects, and soliciting donations as methods to reach the goal.

share with the church family, **OR** have each person *circle* one or two talents from their list generated in Apply.

You may need to help translate some of the gifts into a way the teen can become involved in the church. Explain that they won't necessarily be called upon right away, but that you'll share this list with people in the church who may involve them in the future. Examples:

- Provide or help with music
- Help teach younger children
- Lead recreation during Bible School (sports-minded youth)
- Do a dramatic interpretation of Scripture, reader's theater, tell a story (youth in drama or forensics)
- Do worship movement (someone in ballet or modern dance)
- Lead worship
- Help with minor church repairs (a mechanically-inclined person)
- Make banners or worship centers for the sanctuary (artistic people)
- Contribute to the offering (tithing, for those who have jobs)
- Serve on committees
- Be a junior advisor to middle school groups
- Develop or participate in an outreach ministry that is ongoing
- Start or maintain a recycling or composting program at church
- Other ideas...

If you used the poster paper, put the puzzle pieces back together—either on the bulletin board, or have another heavy paper board along to glue them to. Keep this in the room as a reminder of their gifts and commitments.

Whether you use the puzzle idea or simply circle the items on the list, give a copy of the list to church leaders who can follow through on involving the youth.

INSIGHTS FROM SCRIPTURE

Jesus' parable of the talents is an "easy read," to a point. Mostly, it makes sense. One servant was given over $5,000 (one talent > $1,000). Another servant received $2,000. A third got $1,000.

Each servant, based on his initiative and attitude, did what he felt was best with what he'd been given. The master was quite pleased with the two who had found ways to invest and increase what they had been given. But the third servant was afraid to do anything, hoping just to give back to the master the initial amount. That didn't go over very well. The master got angry, gave the third servant a severe tongue-lashing, and then took away the thousand dollars, too.

That's where it gets a bit uncomfortable for us readers. Okay, so the guy didn't invest his money. He didn't lose it either. Give him a

> **LOOK AHEAD**
> Familiarize yourself with the story in next session's Focus, so you can tell it rather than read it. Also, collect sales fliers or catalogs for everyone. Prepare youth doing role plays in Explore the Bible *Option A* by contacting them prior to the session. You'll need some supplies for the Pictionary activity if using *Option B* in Explore the Bible.

break! But Jesus' words are loud and clear: "For all those who have, more will be given, and they will have an abundance; but from those who have nothing, even what they have will be taken away."

"Talents" has double meaning

Although talents refers to money in this story, the parable can also apply to skills, abilities, things we do well. Surely God is as interested in the ways we invest ourselves as in the ways we invest our financial resources. The reign of God needs the time and energies of many people—people of all ages and abilities, youth included.

Youth may not be standing at the pastor's door, begging to be involved. But many of them, when asked to share themselves in a specific manner, will respond beautifully. They will rise to the occasion of being asked and entrusted with a job, much like the two servants in the parable. Our role as leaders is to help the youth understand that God wants them involved in kingdom-building—in fact, expects it from them. Our role also is to model what it means to be a "good and faithful servant." The fact that you're leading this group is surely a part of your stewardship of your talents!

> This is a story about four people named Everybody, Somebody, Anybody, and Nobody. There was an important job to be done and Everybody was asked to do it. Everybody was sure that Somebody would do it. Anybody could have done it, but Nobody did it. Somebody got angry about that because it was Everybody's job. Everybody thought Anybody could do it but Nobody realized that Everybody wouldn't do it. It ended up that Everybody blamed Somebody when Nobody did what Anybody could have done. The end.

CARLOS

Carlos and his father were car shopping one day, and while they were there, they noticed that the dealership was having a drawing for a new Camaro. Since a person had to be 18 to win the car, Carlos's father entered. "If I win, you can have the car," his father jokingly promised.

You guessed it. Carlos's father won! And he kept his promise to Carlos, who was now the proud owner of a brand new red Camaro.

Carlos drove the car home and parked it in the garage. He didn't drive it again for almost a year. He got it out for the prom, and then the Camaro went back into the garage for another year.

Carlos's friends couldn't believe it. When they asked him why he didn't drive his car, he'd say, "It's just too nice. I'm afraid of it getting damaged."

MANDY

In eleventh grade, Mandy already had college coaches coming to watch her play basketball. She could do it all, but she was particularly deadly with her 3-point shots.

One evening, after a game, the coach from a college that Mandy was seriously considering talked to her. "Come to our basketball camp this summer," the coach said. "You're good enough right now that I could give you a scholarship. Keep working on your game, and you can probably earn a full ride."

Mandy didn't go to the basketball camp that summer, and no one knew why not. She didn't practice her 3-pointers like she had for many summers before. The next year, she played halfheartedly. No one knew why.

DAMIEN

Damien thought that Alicia was just about the best-looking, most fun, sweetest girl in the world. At least the world that he'd seen! He told his friends he'd give anything for a date with her, but he didn't have the nerve to ask.

Then one day, she asked him! She said her youth group was having a Valentine's banquet, and everyone was supposed to bring someone they'd like to get to know better. She wondered if he'd go with her.

Damien asked if he could think about it for a day, and the next day he told her "no thanks." He didn't give her a reason, but he told his friends he just "wasn't good enough" to go out with the girl of his dreams.

ALLISON

Allison had been waiting for her paycheck so she could go buy the latest CD of her favorite artist. She bought it, listened to it once, and then put it away. A week later, she listened to it again. She didn't tell anyone, but she'd decided she could only listen to it once a week, because she was afraid it would get scratched or wear out.

SESSION 3

I'D LIKE TO BE RICH

KEY VERSE
Jesus looked around and said to his disciples, "How hard it will be for those who have wealth to enter the kingdom of God!" (Mark 10:23)

FAITH STORY
Mark 10:17-27

FAITH FOCUS
A wealthy, pious man asked Jesus how to win eternal life. Though the man had kept all the commandments, Jesus required yet more of him; that he sell all he had, give the money to the poor, and follow the Christ-way. This was too much for the man, whose wealth held him back from entering that gate of heaven.

SESSION GOAL
Open young people's eyes to the fact that they are rich in many ways, and that wealth can hinder them from following Jesus.

TEACHING PLAN

1. FOCUS
5-7 minutes

Option A: Tell the following story. If you can, *tell* it rather than read it.

Materials needed and advance preparation
1. Learn the story if you're going to tell it in Focus.
2. Writing paper and pens/pencils
3. Contact youth to do role plays (*option* in Explore)
4. Chalkboard/chalk or newsprint/markers
5. Slips of paper and a container to put them in for Pictionary (*option* in Explore)
6. Bibles
7. Catalogs or sales fliers for everyone
8. Bookmarks made from reproducible sheet for session 3

A large clothing manufacturer in the United States decided to open up a plant in Mexico because the cost of labor was much less there, and it was easy to find people willing to work. So, after building a new facility, they began to hire people, mostly women, to run the sewing machines.

The new employees were good workers, and they were happy with their wages, even though they were making much less than factory people do in the States. The company executives were quite pleased with how things were going, and started talking about opening up some more factories in Mexico.

But before they did, problems came up. Women who were well-trained and doing a good job started quitting. Thinking they'd heard about better money elsewhere, the company increased the employees' wages. But it didn't seem to make any difference. The workers stayed for a while, then quit.

This was driving the executives crazy, so they hired a consultant to go in and find out what was going on. The consultant interviewed the women and asked: "What's wrong? Don't you like the work? Are the conditions bad? Why are you quitting?"

The answers she got were very similar. Everyone was happy with the job and the money they'd made. But once they'd made enough money to pay off their debts, they wanted to be back home with their families. "Why should we spend our lifetime away from our families?" they said. "We made enough to pay our bills, maybe do some improvements on our homes, but that's all we need. Now we want to be back at home with our children."

The consultant thought about what she'd heard, and then contacted the executives. She explained that she'd figured out what the problem was, and that for a large sum of money, she could solve it for them.

The executives were skeptical, but neither did they have any solutions. Finally, they agreed to pay the fee to the consultant.

Before long, all of the employees and former employees received a package, and in it was a big book. And sure enough, within a few weeks, they started coming back. And they kept on returning until the company had all the employees it needed, and people waiting to be hired.

What was the "magic book"? A Sears catalog.

Option B: Using the same story, assign the parts and have the youth pantomime the actions as you tell the story. People needed: executives, employees, consultant.

2. CONNECT
10-12 minutes

Ask the group: *What happened in the story? Why did the women go back to work after getting a catalog?*

Pass out sales fliers or catalogs, and tell youth they have $50-$100 to spend (choose the exact amount depending on the type of fliers or catalogs). Have them circle the things they'd like to buy from the flier or catalog. Then share your "purchases" with the group. If you wish, make a master list on the chalkboard or newsprint.

3. EXPLORE THE BIBLE
10-15 minutes

Shift to this activity by saying: *So what if we want things? Is there anything wrong with that? And what if we happen to be successful and have a lot of money and stuff? Is there something wrong with that? Somebody else was asking questions like that about 2000 years ago.*

Option A: Get volunteers and/or assign the following roles to play in acting out Mark 10:17-27: Reporter, Jesus, a guy named Rich, disciples. Choose your most outgoing, animated (yet thoughtful) person as the reporter.

The skit begins with Rich walking through the room, head down, obviously dejected. The reporter stops Rich and asks him what hap-

---

GENERATION Y sees wealth and wants it...

In 1974 the average U.S. CEO's income was 34 times that of an average worker. In 1995 that average for the CEOs has jumped to 179 times that of an average worker. In comparison to other leading industrialized nations, in 1995 German CEOs got 21 times more than the average blue collar worker and the Japanese topdogs got 20 times more. What do CEOs do that merits this incredible discrepancy?

Jedd Schrock, student

pened—why he's so depressed. Rich tells him about his encounter with Jesus, and what Jesus told him. (Rich will need to be familiar with the story and/or refer to it as he's interviewed.)

Reporter thanks Rich and goes looking for Jesus to get his side of the story. He asks Jesus what happened, and Jesus tells him. Again, the person portraying Jesus needs to know the story.

Reporter seems confused by what Jesus has said, and goes to the disciples to see if they can provide clarification. Reporter asks disciples what Jesus told them, and they repeat what they heard.

Now ask the whole group what the reporter's story should be. What happened here today?

Option B: Pictionary. *Important: Don't let the group know ahead of time what the Bible passage is for this session!*

Divide the group into teams of 3-4. Teams take turns picking pieces of paper from a bowl/hat/whatever, then one team member draws the scene while their team members guess it. (Teams are guessing the particular scene, not the whole story.) Scenes to write on the slips of paper:

- Sell your possessions.
- Give your money to the poor.
- "Teacher, how can I get to heaven?"
- He walked away depressed.

- It's hard for rich people to enter God's kingdom.
- Easier for a camel to get through a needle than a rich person to get into God's kingdom.

First allow one minute to draw. If a group hasn't yet guessed the scene, allow a group that *has* finished to help until all the scenes have been drawn. Then have the group put the scenes together in the order that they happened, *without* looking at the Bible. Once that's done, check it with Mark 10:17-27.

Share background about this story from Insights from Scripture. Discuss it with the group, tying in the story of the Mexican workers.

4. APPLY
7-10 minutes

Option A: Call attention back to the items each person circled in their sales flier or catalog. Ask everyone to imagine that they, like Rich, are asking Jesus what they have that is standing between them and God's kingdom. Is there anything on their "want list" that fits that category? What else might Jesus be saying to them?

Option B: Refer the youth to the story of the factory in Mexico. Ask them: *What is your "Sears catalog"? In other words, what in your life may be keeping you from giving your time and attention to the important things of life? What are those important things for you?* You may need to help differentiate between their needs and their wants.

> Our beds are empty 2/3 of the time.
> Our living rooms are empty 7/8 of the time.
> Our office buildings are empty 1/2 the time.
> It's time we gave this some thought.
>
> R. Buckminster Fuller, inventor of the geodesic dome and proponent of doing more with less

> Happiness doesn't come from having things, it comes from being part of things.

5. RESPOND
5 minutes

Option A: Hand out the bookmarks copied from the reproducible sheet. Ask youth to fill in the center portion of the bookmark. Encourage them to keep the bookmark where it'll remind them of what they talked about in this session.

Option B: Refer once again to the catalogs or sales fliers. Ask youth to tear out an item similar to one they currently have or would like to have, AND that they are willing to "devalue" in their lives. Examples: CD's—do they need so many? Clothes—can they buy less? Do they have to be "name brand"?

Conclude with this prayer or choose one of your own:

Generous God,
show us the way to live beyond our means, and into your kingdom. AMEN.

INSIGHTS FROM SCRIPTURE

A young man came to Jesus, wondering what he'd have to do to inherit eternal life. Jesus listed the commandments, and the man said, "Yes! I've done all that!" Then, instead of patting him on the back, Jesus said, "One more thing. Go sell your stuff, give the money to the poor, and then come along with me."

Not exactly what the man wanted to hear. What? Give up all he's worked for? The big house? The nice clothes? Everything? Give it all up to become a homeless disciple? Not on your life.

And therein, he probably lost his hope for life eternal. Wealth stood between the man and his commitment to the kingdom of heaven. His possessions were of most importance to him.

In the opinion of *The Interpreter's Bible*, Jesus was not laying down the rule that poverty is a requirement, or even the ideal, for his followers. Rather, it was the answer for *this* man who valued his material possessions too greatly. As a good physician, Jesus had diagnosed the problem, and prescribed the cure—the action that would free him from whatever was holding him back from total commitment. In this case it was wealth, yes, but also the man's emotional and spiritual attachment to it.

Many of us North Americans may, at this point, say to ourselves, "No problem. I'm not rich, so this doesn't apply to me." Not true. Most of us are rich, compared to the majority of the world's population. We have all we need and much more.

"Okay, so I'm rich. But I'm not attached to it, so this story still doesn't really hit me where I am."

Maybe. Maybe not. That's something for each of us to search out within our souls. Chances

> **LOOK AHEAD**
>
> For next session, *Option A* in Connect will require pieces of paper prepared before the session, each with the name of someone who's a good steward on it. *Option A* in Explore the Bible calls for someone to do a dramatic portrayal of the good Samaritan. You will need a watch, $10 bill, sterile gloves, and a Bible for *Option B* in Apply.

are, we will find ourselves more attached than we want to believe we are.

The problem with wealth

After the rich man left, Jesus recognized a "teachable moment" with his disciples. "How hard it will be for those who have riches to enter the kingdom of God!" he says. The disciples were shocked! In this statement, Jesus contradicted the Old Testament idea and rabbinical teachings that prosperity is a blessing on the righteous. They'd never heard this teaching before.

Jesus didn't go into details or explain why. He seemed to say, "Take my word for it." But if he'd offered an explanation, it might have included the following: Abundance is an enemy to the true "abundant life." Relationships with God and other people are what really matter in life. The problem with wealth is that it can easily become more important than people or God's kingdom. Of course, poverty can function the same way. Security becomes wrapped up in things and money. Being poor does not automatically mean that priorities are in order. And it's not *impossible* to be rich *and* have priorities in order. But it's downright hard.

How hard? Jesus painted a graphic picture for the disciples. "It is easier for a camel to go through the eye of a needle than for someone who is rich to enter the kingdom of God."

WHAT?

For centuries, scholars have struggled with that one. There are those who've tried to explain it by saying that Jesus meant a "needle's eye" gate—a small gate beside the large city gate; and that a loaded camel had to get on its knees to go through. Thus, say these scholars, we must enter the kingdom of heaven—on our knees.

Opponents of that theory laugh it off, saying the gate was too small for a camel loaded or unloaded, standing or kneeling; and besides, whoever saw a camel crawling on its knees?

Most scholars, instead, say that Jesus was simply using hyperbole—major exaggeration just for the effect of it. Maybe, when we read the story in the Bible, we don't have the advantage of seeing the twinkle in Jesus' eye that his disciples could see.

Bottom line? If we are to follow Christ, he demands our undivided allegiance. We must do significant soul-searching to determine how our riches are getting in the way.

Session 4

A MAN WITH AN ATTITUDE

Materials needed and advance preparation
1. Wet-wipes, snack food, a blanket, pillow, magazines—anything else a steward might give to passengers on a plane (*Option A* in Focus)
2. Small pieces of paper (and tape and pins), each with the name of a person who's a good steward (*Option A* in Connect)
3. Recruit someone to do a dramatic portrayal of the good Samaritan (*Option A* in Explore).
4. Watch, $10 bill, sterile gloves, Bible (*Option B* in Apply)
5. "Hat," paper, and timer (*Option C* in Apply)
6. Bibles
7. Chalkboard/chalk, or newsprint/marker

KEY VERSES
[The Samaritan] went to [the wounded man] and bandaged his wounds, having poured oil and wine on them. Then he put him on his own animal, brought him to an inn, and took care of him. The next day [the Samaritan] took out two denarii, gave them to the innkeeper, and said, "Take care of him; and when I come back, I will repay you whatever more you spend." (Luke 10:34-35)

FAITH STORY
Luke 10:25-37

FAITH FOCUS
A traveler who was mugged on the dangerous road to Jericho got help from an unexpected source. The familiar story of the good Samaritan highlights elements of good stewardship: attitude, willingness to take risks, and a generous offering of time and money.

SESSION GOAL
Build awareness in youth that stewardship is a lifestyle, a response to God's reaching out to us.

TEACHING PLAN

1. FOCUS
6-8 minutes

Option A: Set the room up with rows of chairs similar to what you'd see in a plane (2-3 chairs on either side with an aisle in the middle.) Ask or assign a person to be the "steward." The rest of the youth are passengers in the make-believe plane. The passengers may ask the steward/flight attendant to do everything from feeding them to washing their faces. (Encourage the youth to have some fun with this!) Provide the steward with wet-wipes, snack foods, blanket, pillow, magazines—other things they might give to people on a plane. The point is to get youth to notice that the way of life of a steward is to care for others.

Option B: Make a list of names of people that might be considered good stewards. Include famous names as well as people in your church and community. Suggestions: Martin Luther King Jr., Gandhi, Jimmy Carter (Habitat for Humanity), Terry Fox (ran across Canada to raise money for cancer research), Mother Theresa, Nellie McClung (women's rights activist), Sir Frederick Banting (co-discoverer of insulin), Harriet Tubman (a builder of the "Underground Railroad"). Get enough names for each youth in the group, and put the names on individual pieces of paper. Then stick a paper on the back of each person, and ask youth to mingle and ask each other yes/no questions until everyone has guessed whose name they have. (Note: If you have a very small group, repeat this game several times until you have named at least six people.)

2. CONNECT
7-10 minutes

Next, ask the youth to:

1. Define what it means to be a good steward.
2. Define the word stewardship.

Follow up by asking if Donald Trump should be on the list of good stewards. After hearing their opinions, tell or read the following true story.

> A limousine was parked along the side of the road with a flat tire, and a passing motorist stopped to see if he could be of assistance. He ended up helping change the tire. Just before he got into his car to leave, the window of the limousine rolled down, and Donald Trump said, "Thank you so much for helping us. What can I pay you?" The man said, "My wife's at home waiting for me. Just send her a big bouquet of flowers—that's all the thanks I need, and she'd really appreciate it."
>
> The next day the bouquet of flowers arrived at their home. Along with it was a note that said, "We took care of your house mortgage as well."

Now ask: *Who was a good steward in this story?* (You may get votes for both characters.)

3. EXPLORE THE BIBLE
10 minutes

Shift to this activity by saying: *A common expression for what the passing motorist did when he helped change the tire is "being a good Samaritan." Let's go back in time to that original good Samaritan.*

Option A: Ask someone in your congregation or someone else you know who would do a dramatic portrayal of the good Samaritan. Have him come to the session and tell the story from the Samaritan's perspective. Some things to cover:

- *Why did he stop and help?*
- *Wasn't he afraid of being robbed, too? (Maybe the robbers were just waiting for someone to stop.)*
- *Did this make him late for where he was going?*
- *Why did he spend his hard-earned money on the guy?*
- *What kind of recognition did he get for his good deed?*

Option B: Ask one of the youth to read the following "Multiple Choice Story," one number at a time, and have the other youth guess the answer.

- A good steward—someone who feels responsible for and cares for other people, for the environment, and for anything entrusted to him or her.
- Biblical stewardship—giving a hand up any time it is needed; putting your own needs aside to help out another.
- Stewardship—living all of life as if it is a gift.
- Simple life—one that has sharp focus and clear purpose.

GENERATION Y and their cash:
- Average teen's personal income: $3,692
- Average weekly allowance for 13- to 15-year-old boys: $15.25; for girls: $16.90
- Teens who work part- or full-time: 37%
- Average amount teens spend per week: $66

from *React*, January 1996

1. A man was taking a hike down the road from Jerusalem to Jericho. This road was:
   a. a freeway.
   b. pretty decent, as roads went in those days.
   c. about 17 miles long.
   d. major steep and rocky—dropped 3400 feet in altitude.

2. Along that famous road, there were:
   a. rocks, rocks and more rocks.
   b. Call for Help boxes.
   c. Golden Arches.
   d. mean and nasty robbers.

3. The robbers beat up the traveler, stole his clothes and money, and:
   a. made sure he was dead.
   b. figured he would die.
   c. called 911.
   d. warned him not to start screaming until he'd counted to 100.

4. The robbers left. The man thought he was dead. A preacher came walking by. The preacher:
   a. took one look and hightailed it out of there.
   b. said, "I'll go get help."
   c. immediately bent down and began to help the wounded man.
   d. said, "I'm really sorry, but I have a meeting and I can't be late."

5. Another religious leader showed up along the road. He saw the guy who'd been clobbered. So he:
   a. yelled at the preacher to come back and do something.
   b. got out his handy-dandy First Aid kit and did what he could to help the guy.
   c. prayed for him.
   d. said to himself, "I didn't see that," and just kept right on walking.

6. A Samaritan rode up on a donkey. Middle-class guy on a business trip. He too saw the bruised and bleeding traveler. And he:
   a. said, "What on earth happened? Here—I've got a First Aid kit—let's see what we can do for you."
   b. looked at his watch, realized he didn't have time to stop, and hurried on.
   c. promised to send an ambulance out from Jericho as soon as he got there.

7. After loading the injured man on his donkey, the Good Guy took him to a mospital. (That's right, a combination motel and hospital.) There he:
   a. told the mospital people he'd done all he could, and he'd appreciate it if they'd take over now.
   b. asked for a room for the two of them, and made sure the guy was okay through the night.

8. The next morning, the Good Guy left. But first, he:
   a. made arrangements with the local church to come and help the injured traveler.
   b. contacted the traveler's insurance company.

c. paid the mospital for services rendered, and said he'd pay any more bills that came up.

Whichever option you used, read the story from the Bible as well (Luke 10:25-37). Then suggest that this is more than the story of a good Samaritan—it's the story of a good steward. The outward signs are that he gave his time and his money to help the wounded man. He wouldn't have had to give either one, but he did. Why? Because his attitude toward life was in the right place. He wasn't selfish. He was willing to give, even when that meant taking risks.

4. APPLY
10-12 minutes

Option A: Ask youth to imagine the following: It's 100 years from now. A group of teenagers from this church is studying this very topic. The leader has written your name on a piece of paper as one of the "people in the past" the church remembers as a good steward. Why? What are they remembering about you?

Option B: Pass the following items around the group—a watch, a pair of plastic gloves, a $10 bill, a Bible. These represent time, risk, money, and attitude, respectively. As each person gets an object, they state, on a scale of 1 (*Great!*) to 5 (*lots of room to improve*) how they're doing as a steward in that area. Examples:

- "I'd give 'time' a 5 because I always seem too busy to help somebody else."
- "For me, the money isn't so hard. I'd give it a difficulty of 1. I can give money easier than time."
- "I'm afraid of taking risks. I'd give that a 4."
- "I believe all this stuff, so I think my attitude is a good 2."

Option C: Divide the group into two sides. Put the following four categories on the chalkboard or newsprint for the group to see: Time, Money, Risk, Attitude. Have four pieces of paper in a "hat" for them to take turns drawing from—the papers are labeled Time, Money, Risk and Attitude. When a team draws a category, they have 15 seconds to come up with a specific thing a person could do in that area to improve their stewardship. Time and Money categories are worth 2 points, Risk and Attitude categories are worth 5 points. If the team succeeds, they can draw again until they don't come up with an answer in 15 seconds. Then it's the other team's turn. After a response is given, the paper goes back in the hat and can be drawn again. You act as judge. The team with the most points at the end of 5 minutes wins.

5. RESPOND
5-7 minutes

Option A: Ask youth to fill in the following sentence prayer as you go around the group: "God, help me to be a good steward in the area of _____."

> Good stewardship does not mean tithing as much as it is concerned with what you do with the rest of the 90% of your resources.
>
> Anna Mow,
> Brethren churchwoman

LOOK AHEAD

Option A in Focus of session 5 requires having a small party for part of the group prior to the session. *Option B* in Focus requires contacting a few youth prior to the session.

You'll need to write party invitations for each person: "God is inviting you to a party. Please RSVP."

Option B: Lead the group in prayer, asking God to be with each person as they learn what it means to be a good steward. If you feel comfortable with it, pray out loud for each young person, particularly if they've mentioned a kind of stewardship in which they either "do well" or "need work." If you need to take notes as they're talking so you can pray specifically for them, be prepared to do that when they're sharing.

INSIGHTS FROM SCRIPTURE

A traveler was held up, robbed, beaten almost to the point of death, and left by the side of the road to die. Along came a religious leader—someone you'd expect to "practice what he preaches." This preacher took one look at the bloody mess, shuddered, and hurried on. Another religious-type arrived on the scene. Same story.

Finally, help arrived for the dying traveler in the form of a Samaritan. He didn't fit into the religious norms of the community. Didn't go to the "right" church. But he saw someone desperately in need, and he didn't think twice. He applied what First Aid he could with what he had available. Then he took the person to a place where he could rest, recuperate, and be cared for. Even then, he didn't leave. He spent the night with the traveler, caring for him until the next day when he went on his way.

But that wasn't all. The Samaritan made a downpayment on the traveler's hospitalization costs and said, "I'll be back to pay whatever else is owed for his care."

What an incredible example of stewardship! Let's look at his attitude, his willingness to take risks, and his use of his time and money.

Attitude

This story is one of many ways that Jesus emphasized the importance of love for each other—not a love out of duty or out of knowing we will be loved in return, but a love that flows freely out of our being as a response to the love of God within us. From the admonition to go the second mile to the great banquet for the prodigal son, Jesus' teachings are saturated with this theme.

Many of us have grown up with the impression that stewardship is synonymous with (a) money, and (b) a duty to give a tithe. No! Stewardship is not a school assignment that we have to do to please the teacher. Rather, stewardship is an attitude, a lifestyle, a response to God's goodness, a celebration of the abundance of gifts God has given us!

Risk-taking

If we came upon a bleeding person alongside the road today, many of us would ask ourselves, "Am I willing to take the risk to help? What about AIDS?" Certainly the Samaritan was aware of risks. Maybe the robbers who got this guy were waiting behind the rocks to nail *him*. Maybe the guy would die, and someone would come along and accuse him of being the killer. After all, they didn't like Samaritans around there.

Stewardship scares us. We're afraid that in giving, we'll lose. We don't want to take the risk. In reality, the rewards make the risks worth taking.

Time

Did the religious leaders that passed by the wounded man have important church meetings they needed to get to? Maybe. The Samaritan surely had places to be and things to do, too. But he not only stopped and transported the traveler—he spent the night and cared for him until the next day.

Adults and teens alike seem too often to be crazy-busy. School and work commitments eat up the hours, and if they don't, television and videos provide great ways to fill our time. What if we'd evaluate how we use our time, even our vocation, with the following question: "How will this help bring in God's kingdom?"

Money

Did the Samaritan calculate his monthly income and leave exactly ten percent with the innkeeper? No. The "man with the attitude" simply saw a need and paid what was required to meet the need. He left two days' compensation with the innkeeper, and then promised to pay whatever else was owed when he returned.

What does that mean for us? It means we start somewhere—10% is one possibility. The tithe has often been used as a standard amount to give. Traditionally, it was the "first fruits" of any harvest. The tithe would be given first, and what was *left over* would be used for personal use.

Personally, I like the idea of starting with 10% and increasing it by 1% every year. That's one formula. It's amazing to see what happens in the process of slowly increasing the percentage.

Up until now, we've promoted stewardship as an *attitude* out of which *actions* are the result. The area of money is no different. However, I'd like to suggest that there is a place here for us to experiment in reverse. Take the *action*—JUST DO IT—and see if the attitude doesn't follow. Live beyond your means. Give a certain percentage to a cause you feel good about, and see if you don't find yourself rejoicing and happy to be a good steward of money.

Will this be a "tough sell" for teenagers? With so many "wants" demanding their money, it might be. Helping them to find a tangible place/people to give their "God-money" to is part of the solution. It's more rewarding to give to a specific cause than to a nebulous general fund. Reminding them of the "Sears catalog syndrome" from session 3 may help clarify priorities. God has given us much. Giving of ourselves, our time, and our money stems from an attitude that is right with God. Stewardship is a lifestyle—it's how we respond to all of life.

> In the early church, the offering meant presenting the bread and communion wine for consecration. They were gifts brought by people to be used in the worship of God. Today, offering usually means presenting financial gifts. Though the gifts have changed, bringing them to God still ought to be a highlight of worship.

> There's more joy in giving when there are more people giving. That's not only because the load is shared, but because the group gets to know that giving is a thing the group does together. Knowing that I belong to a generous church makes me more generous.
>
> Bud Farrar,
> Church of the Brethren

Session 5

PARTY ON!

Materials needed and advance preparation
1. Stage a small party for part of the group (*Option A* in Focus).
2. Contact youth prior to the session to stage the aftermath of a party (*Option B* in Focus).
3. Party invitations (one per person) on which you've written: *God is inviting you to a party. Please RSVP.*
4. Reproducible sheets for session 5
5. Bibles

KEY VERSES
Then Jesus said to [the dinner guest], "Someone gave a great dinner and invited many. At the time for the dinner he sent his slave to say to those who had been invited, 'Come; for everything is ready now.' But they all alike began to make excuses." (Luke 14:16-18a)

FAITH STORY
Luke 14:12-24

FAITH FOCUS
Jesus told a parable about a "great dinner," in which a person invited many friends to a lavish party. When the day of the dinner came, however, the invited guests all sent excuses for why they couldn't attend. So the host, angry, instead brought the poor, the lame, and the blind to enjoy the feast.

Jesus insisted that showing hospitality to those who could not repay the favor would result in God's blessing.

SESSION GOAL
Invite youth to accept God's gifts and to live as if they know they've received great blessings.

TEACHING PLAN

1. FOCUS
3-5 minutes

Option A: Stage a party for just part of the group, and tell them it's a secret from the other youth in the group. Do this either prior to the session (invite several kids to come early for food and fun) or on another day. It doesn't have to be a big deal—the object is to end up in this session with some people who were at the party and can talk about it and others who weren't. At the beginning of this session, talk about the party with the youth who were there. Play it up. Find ways to make the others jealous that they weren't there.

Option B: A fictitious variation on *Option A*. Contact several youth ahead of time and ask them to be the first ones to the session. They are to be talking about a fictitious party that they were at the evening before, making it sound like a lot of fun and something that the other youth will wish they'd been at too. If/when the others ask them about it, they should simply say they had a lot of fun, and it's too bad the others missed it.

Option C: Ask youth to close their eyes and imagine the following scenario as you tell it.

(Tell it slowly, allowing time for them to imagine what's happening.)

Imagine that someone you like a lot is throwing a party, and you're really looking forward to going to it. The morning of the party, you get the flu. Bad. You feel horrible, and you know you're not going anywhere. That evening, while you're dead in bed, your friends are having a great time.

The next day, you feel good enough to go back to school. Your friends are all talking about the fun they had at the party. What are you thinking as you hear them talk? What are you feeling?

2. CONNECT
7-10 minutes

Whether you used Option A, B, or C in the Focus, talk about it with the youth. How does it feel to have missed the party? Do they regret not being there? Why? Is it because other people got in on some fun that they didn't?

Hand out the invitations that say: *God is inviting you to a party. Please RSVP.*

Say to the youth, *Assuming that this invitation is for real, you don't have any questions about whether or not it's a joke, and you know where the party's being held, what will your RSVP be? Yes? No? Not sure? (Would it be boring? What **kind** of party would it be?)* Go around the group and hear everyone's RSVP.

3. EXPLORE THE BIBLE
10-15 minutes
Shift to this activity by saying:
Believe it or not, that invitation is for real. Let's see how some other people have chosen to RSVP to it.

Hand out the reproducible sheets and assign one person to each part. You may want to take a part, too.

Optional: Read the story from Luke 14:16-24 as well.

Discuss the reasons given by the six people for not going, plus those given by the youth during the Connect section. Ask them how they think the reasons are similar to the reasons people use not to adopt stewardship as a lifestyle. See what kinds of answers the youth come up with before offering the following:

John, Ben, and Juanita all thought they had better things to do with their time. Stewardship involves spending our lives to "further the kingdom of God." Stewardship is an attitude. It means living as if we know we have received a great gift from God, and are eager to share it with others because there's so much.

Kristi and Kyrene were afraid to take a chance on something they didn't know. We're afraid to risk giving a percentage of our money, for example. Antoine's concern was money as well—he didn't want to "lose" any of it.

GENERATION Y has ideas about how to spend time...
- watching TV: 68% say they do it too much, 27% say they do it too little
- praying: 86% say they do it too little
- helping others: 18% say they do it too much, and 76% say they don't do enough
- studying: 19% say they do it too much, and 74% say they do too little of it

Excerpted from a 1995 Gallup youth survey

4. APPLY
7-10 minutes

Ask youth to open their party invitations and write a *specific* RSVP to God's party. In Connect, you already talked about their *reaction* to the invitation. Now challenge them to show how they might live as if they are part of God's party by trying out stewardship in at least one way in their life. Some things they may be willing to do:

- Volunteer in church or community.
- Begin giving a certain percentage of income.
- Commit to thinking twice and praying before making purchases.
- Sign up for summer voluntary service assignment.
- Watch where you shop and what you buy. Where do the products come from? (See sidebar on *Shopping for a Better World.*)
- Buy clothes at a secondhand store. Use the money saved to help someone else.
- Rethink the way they spend time and change some priorities. Make a prayer center as outlined in the extender session, *Option B.*
- Visit someone in a nursing home on a regular basis.
- Recycle.
- Teach children's Sunday school or Vacation Bible School.
- Commit to pray daily for a missionary family.
- Think about what kinds of jobs you'll take in light of what is good stewardship (see sidebar on Pledge of Social and Environmental Responsibility).

> Generation Y takes risks and enjoys excitement, but in many cases wouldn't look to their spiritual lives and/or church community to provide it.

> In the past few years the following Pledge of Social and Environmental Responsibility has caught on at commencement ceremonies: "I pledge to investigate and take into account the social and environmental consequences of any job opportunity I consider." Some students sign and keep a wallet-size card stating the pledge, while students and supportive faculty wear green ribbons at commencement, with the pledge being printed in the formal commencement program. The pledge helps educate and motivate students to contribute to a better world, and can be a focal point for other types of consciousness-raising both on and off campus.

Encourage youth to think of something they really are willing to try, but at the same time, respect their position if they aren't ready to make a commitment. Ask them to share their commitments, giving freedom to "pass" if they wish.

5. RESPOND
5-15 minutes

Option A: Plan a stewardship "event" the group can do together. This could include:

- a service project.
- deciding on a project to give money toward, and committing as a group to bring a percentage of their income for the project.
- for really ambitious groups, sharing this look at stewardship with the rest of the congregation through a Youth Sunday or a workshop.

Option B: Lead the group in the following directed prayer:

Our generous God, thank you for the many gifts you have given us:
    for the people who are important to us (pause);
    for possessions (pause);
    for homes (pause);
    for money (pause);
    for skills and talents (pause).
God, help us know how we can give ourselves back to your kingdom, in the areas of:
    the people we relate to (pause);
    the things we own (pause);
    money (pause);

time (pause);

abilities (pause).

God, thank you for inviting us to your party. Help us get past all the things that might make it hard for us to say, "Yes! I'll be there!" (pause) *In the name of Jesus, who truly showed us how to live beyond our means, AMEN.*

INSIGHTS FROM SCRIPTURE

"Please accept my regrets."
"I cannot come."

With those words, the people in the parable of the great dinner turned down their invitations. Why? What could be more enticing than an elegant free meal?

Apparently a lot of things. According to commentary from *The Interpreter's Bible*, the three excuses give a picture of a successful secular society. The farm symbolizes possessions and investments; the oxen and plow, our technological ways of making a living; the wife, our human-centered comfort, including sex.

These things aren't bad or wrong in and of themselves. But when they become more important than an invitation from God, we've got a problem with priorities, and with our understanding of what the abundant life is all about.

Are we afraid the banquet will be dull? That this "stewardship lifestyle" won't be fun?

That we may not have enough if we truly live beyond our means? We're more likely to trust money, possessions, technology and sexual fulfillment for our happiness than the unknown at God's party.

Money, possessions, technology, sex. Sound like anything your youth are interested in? How are we supposed to help them say yes! to God's party when the world is not just inviting, but at times coercing youth to feast on those things?

Be an example, for starters. We can tell our own stories—both successes and struggles—with stewardship. We can talk about what's happened in our lives when we gave of our time, talents, and money to God. We can testify to the fact that the banquet not only *isn't* dull, but that it fulfills our lives. We are happier when we can live fulfilled lives, and it's fun to be happy!

Second, we can invite youth to go to the banquet with us. It's one thing to say, "I went, it was great, you ought to go too." It's another thing to say, "I'll pick you up and we'll go together."

What might that mean? The list of "things to do" in the Apply section is a start. Pick one or two to do with your group, or with a few youth who are serious about exploring stewardship as lifestyle, about "living beyond our means." Discover your own applications.

We've been invited to a great banquet. The regrets will be ours if we choose not to go.

Resource: *Shopping for a Better World*

This "quick and easy guide to socially responsible supermarket shopping" rates makers of 1600 brand name products on charitable giving, animal testing, environment, defense contracts, women and minority advancement, among others. Put out by the Council on Economic Priorities, Ballantine Books, New York (1989).

There is great joy in living lives grounded in the practices of simple living. It's not only the right thing to do, it's the healthy thing to do.

Just Say No?

TV TALK SHOW HOST: Hello, and welcome to the "What WOULD You Do? Show"—a show where we find out what people did when put in some strange, and some not-so-strange circumstances! Our guests today include six people who were invited to party. Not so unusual, you say? Well, it just so happens the invitations said the party was being given by God. That's right, God. So, John Swartzendruber, what'd you think when you went to the mailbox one day and found this invitation in it?

JOHN: I didn't know what to think. It was corn planting time, and I wasn't thinking about much else. I'd just bought some land that I'd been wanting for a long time, and I was busy getting it ready to put corn in. The party sounded interesting, but when the weather's right, I've got to be in the fields.

HOST: Didn't it say something about a huge smorgasbord meal? You have to eat sometime! Why didn't you go for the food at least?

JOHN: Guess I figured it'd still take up most of the evening. I sent the RSVP back and asked to be excused this time, and I ended up packing a snack and working out in the field that evening.

HOST: Very interesting. Ben Good, how about you? You got an invitation too?

BEN: Yup, I did.

HOST: And?

BEN: Well you see, I'd just been to the Henderson sale that day, and bought me a team of oxen. They looked so good in the sale ring, I couldn't resist, so I bought them. I could hardly wait to get home and see if they worked together as good as they looked. The phone was ringing when I walked in the house. Somebody wanting to confirm that I'd be at the party that evening.

HOST: So you'd already sent in your RSVP and said yes?

BEN: Yup. But that was before I had those oxen. I just had to stay home and try them out. So I told the woman on the phone I wouldn't be there.

HOST: Okay, so you didn't make it either. And now we have Juanita Rodriquez. Juanita, did you go to the party?

JUANITA: I don't think so! That was my wedding day! I had my own party to go to!

HOST: Of course. Well, moving right along. We have some teenagers with us who were invited to the same party. Kids love parties, so let's hear from them. Kristi, tell us your story.

KRISTI: I was going to go. Really I was. It sounded like a lot of fun. But then I got to thinking, what if it's not fun when I get there? I'd never been to one of his parties. I'd hate to show up and have a really rotten time, you know what I mean? So I decided not to take the chance on having a bad time, and I didn't go at all.

HOST: You weren't willing to risk one evening of your time?

KRISTI: I know it sounds stupid now, looking back.

HOST: How about you, young man? Antoine, did you go?

ANTOINE: I had to be working.

HOST: You couldn't get off? Trade with somebody?

ANTOINE: Actually, yeah, I could. I asked my boss, and he said that'd be cool. But I needed the money I made that evening, plus it was payday. Going to the party would've meant making less money, and not getting paid that day. So I didn't go.

HOST: This is wild. Just wild! Everybody had an excuse not to go to the party! How about our final guest, Kyrene? Did you go?

KYRENE: Nope. I didn't know who else would be there. I don't like to try new things. I didn't even consider going.

HOST: Unbelievable. God throws a party, and you've heard from six people with reasons not to go. On tomorrow's show, we'll talk to some folks who *did* make it to God's party. See you then!

Copyright © 1996 by Faith & Life Press and Brethren Press. Permission is granted to photocopy this handout for use with session 5.

EXTENDER SESSION

best used after session 1 (*Option A*) **OR** session 4 (*Option B*)

Option A: STEWARDSHIP OF THE ENVIRONMENT

Session Goal: Help youth translate their concern about environmental issues into a faith issue: Our job as stewards is to take care of that which does not belong to us—God's earth.

Session Plan: Without a doubt, environmental crises are stewardship issues. The earth was God's first gift to humankind, and the health and well-being of our planet is a matter of life and death for we who inhabit it.

Tony Campolo's book is a good one for further study and ideas on this topic (see sidebar). Use this extender option to plan one of the following project possibilities with your youth:

- Start a campaign in your church and/or community for people to USE RECHARGEABLE BATTERIES. The heavy metals in batteries contribute to hazardous wastes. The most common of these dangerous metals is mercury. How dangerous is it? The hatmakers of the 17th century used mercury to treat felt. Since mercury poisons the brain, many of the hatmakers were literally driven crazy, giving birth to the expression "mad as a hatter." Use rechargeable batteries whenever possible. Take orders for batteries and chargers, and see if you can find a place where you can buy them at a discount and re-sell them as a fund-raiser.

- START A CHRISTIAN "RELEAF" CAMPAIGN. Organize "ReLeaf Teams" to go out and plant trees. If every North American would plant a tree, more than a billion pounds of "greenhouse gases" would be removed from the atmosphere every year.

- HOLD "RECYCLE" SALES. Same as a garage sale, but a better name. Emphasizes reusing rather than throwing away.

- OPEN A "RECYCLE STORE." Commonly called a thrift shop, a recycle shop is a necessity for poor people, but also for responsible Christians who want to avoid unnecessary and expensive buying.

- BEGIN A REDUCE-REUSE-RECYCLE PROGRAM at your church. One aspect of this would be for youth to coordinate a recycling program at the church. But even more basic to the issue of stewardship, it would encourage people to reduce their use of our environment's resources. Reduce first, then reuse, and finally recycle.

"What do you think is the most important issue Christians will have to face in the next ten years?" I asked. Four of us...were taking a break from an all-day meeting of evangelical leaders who had gotten together to discuss the future of the church.

Without hesitation, Tom Sine, an outstanding author and futurologist, shot back, "The environment!" The other two immediately agreed. This surprised me since one of those at the table was Ron Sider, author of *Rich Christians in an Age of Hunger*. I thought he would certainly have said something like hunger or poverty. But no! He went on to explain that if the destruction of the environment continues, more and more land will be unavailable to grow food.

Martha Lyon simply commented that the environment had become a primary concern of youth. "Paying attention to the environment," she said, "is something young people make us do."

Tony Campolo, in *How to Rescue the Earth*

Taking care of what's already there

For nearly 15 years the massive old Funk Brothers Seed Co. soybean storage plant sat abandoned in Bloomington, Illinois. "This was a derelict old building, no longer approved for grain storage. There seemed to be absolutely no use for it but it is so solid it would have been extremely difficult to tear (it) down," noted architect Harry Riddle, who helped transform a white elephant into a hot commodity.

The hot commodity? The old Funk Brothers property has been transformed into the Upper Limits Rock Gym, one of the nation's premiere facilities for a hot fitness fad. Four of the plant's 13 silos have been converted so far. They contain 44 roped routes...an outdoor climbing area,...and an ice waterfall for ice climbing enthusiasts. What's next? A 3-story apartment in one of the other silos....

Excerpted from Chicago Tribune article, 1995

Option B: STEWARDSHIP OF TIME

Session Goal: Give youth a strategy for practicing a stewardship of their time, by introducing them to prayerful contemplation and silence.

Session Plan: Another aspect of stewardship is to learn to recognize the presence of God in one's life. Doing this requires setting aside time each day or week for silence and prayer. It may at first be difficult to do, yet we are convinced that our life doesn't work without rest and food, and so we make time for those necessities. We need to model for youth that our spiritual health is no less critical than food and rest. When we regularly spend time "practicing the presence of God," we do not lose time for other things, because God has more freedom to work in our lives and we have more freedom to let God work! This becomes a valuable stewardship of personal time.

Set aside a corner of your meeting place, or even another room in the church building, for quiet and contemplation. Provide candles, perhaps even music, a Bible, other prayer books. Encourage youth to set up their own prayer space at home. Offer to take pledges for the time they will spend: Begin with five minutes per day, or 15 minutes sometime during the week, and gradually increase the time. Use this extender session to sit together in your prayer place, and model what the prayer/contemplation time can be. Spend some time in silence, in prayer, in short readings, in singing.

Psalm 131 is a wonderful prayer to begin meditation.

[1] My heart is not proud, O Lord,
My eyes are not haughty;
I will not concern myself with
great issues,
or with things that are beyond my reach.
[2] I have stilled and quieted my soul;
like a weaned child with its mother,
like a weaned child is my soul within me.
[3] O my heart, put your hope in the Lord
both now and forevermore.

Paraphrase based on NIV

WHAT DID YOU THINK OF THIS GENERATION WHY BIBLE STUDIES UNIT?

Living Beyond Our Means

Your name: _____

Congregation: _____

Approximate number of youth who participated in this study: _____

In what setting did you use this unit?
- ❏ Sunday school
- ❏ camp
- ❏ other
- ❏ youth group
- ❏ retreat

Do you use *With* magazine and *YouthGuide* newsletter, the other two components of the Generation Why package?
- ❏ *With* magazine
- ❏ *YouthGuide* newsletter
- ❏ Both

Name other youth curriculum resources you've used in the past two years:

1. Did this unit address issues of faith and culture relevant to your youth?

2. Did you find the unit to be flexible enough to meet the needs of your group? Why or why not?

3. Would you recommend this unit to another youth leader? Why or why not?

Tell me more about:
- ❏ other Generation Why Bible Studies units
- ❏ *With* magazine
- ❏ *YouthGuide* newsletter

Return this form to the Generation Why Bible Studies office:
34595 Row River Rd.
Cottage Grove, OR 97424